David,

Thank you for sharing your spirit with us. You are a blessing. May the Lord shine on you and lead you in new places.

Kim

Force of the Spirit

Kim Daus-Edwards

A Photographic Canon
By Kim Daus-Edwards

Teach Me   Psalm 25:4

Antique Truck Headlight, Denver, Colorado 1992

Force of the
Spirit

A Photographic Canon
By Kim Daus-Edwards

Force of the Spirit, by Kim Daus-Edwards
© 2005
Photos © Kim Daus-Edwards
Text © Kim Daus-Edwards
All rights reserved

Published by Indaba Publishing
A division of The Institute
Emerald Hills, California

Unless otherwise noted,
Scripture references are from the New International Version.

Library of Congress Cataloging in Publication Data
ISBN: 0-9678541-4-8

First Edition, October 2005

Front Cover:
Kim Daus-Edwards, *I Have Seen You in the Sanctuary*, 1994

Back Cover:
Kim Daus Edwards, *Some Things Are Hidden*, 1993

www.forceofthespirit.com
www.daus.com/photography
www.daus.com

Contents

FORCE OF THE SPIRIT

This collection of images is a chronicle, a storybook. It shows what I have seen, where I have been, people I've met along the way. Through these photographs I share feelings, reflections, and growth. In many ways, this collection represents a surrender to the idea of the holy through the medium of photography.

You might say this photographic canon is also a testament to theology, or my relationship to God. It's how I see the world. Reverence, faith, gratitude. Praise, mystery, wilderness wandering. Worship, sacrifice, covenant, brokenness. Darkness, and the sometimes beauty of it. Confession. Grace, hope, love. The recurring themes. Their movement in life is never still.

I hope that these images are an inspiration, a call, an invitation to answer the force of the Spirit in life, love, work, service, and art. The way we see things and how we respond to our world are our ways to listen and allow the Spirit to speak truth.

In this collection, you'll find the clinging of a soul to its God represented in the arms of a child held by its parents as "soul-of-me." The cry of joy on a young boy's face as pure as joy can be. The deepest longing of body and soul captured in yearning eyes. These images speak of a meaning that draws us closer to God, just as it does if we thirst after Him.

Imagery can help us use more senses to understand the Bible. As we look at Scripture, we see that the Word is layered, cyclical, non-linear at times, unsystematic even, and yet it is soul-filled in a way that validates our lives through the lens of the human story. My hope is that your heart's cries are also reflected in these pictures. Seeing the Word in pictures, just like studying Hebrew or Greek, can open up new dimensions of the text.

Art and the spiritual are inseparable for me--art is about more than sharing in God's sacred act of creation, it is seeing with fresh eyes. I seek to call attention to the sacred through photography. I want to discover and establish values through imagery.

My imagery chronicles the tenacity of the Spirit--the fact that even though we may turn away from it, the Spirit's power is ever-present and emerges regularly in our lives. The Spirit may show itself through ordinary and extraordinary images alike, and these images have helped uncover new layers of my spirit so that I have been able to grow closer to God.

The best images penetrate with an untiring quest for truth. They inspire us to see what we've not seen before. These images require not only participation, but also self-reflection. They invite the viewer to see with new eyes. I share photos and the way I see life because I hope to inspire people to reach out beyond; to reach out toward what seems impossible; to lose oneself to that "beyond," to the Spirit, to Truth. Wonder and awe can die or they can be cultivated and entertained; they can inspire. Each person who opens this book is invited to tap into this Spirit through these photographs.

Photography is a spiritually acute language, but one that can portray a "religionless religion"[1] that can teach us and penetrate a culture. Ansel Adams believed in the power of an image that could capture the spirit of the land. And like Adams, Harry Callahan interpreted the American landscape as "a spiritual and redemptive force, suggesting a relationship between nature and religion and also between photography and religion." [2]

I believe that by following the force of the Spirit, my photography will touch the spirit in others. My prayer is to be faithful to the subjects, and to allow God to use the images, my life, my joy, and creativity in ways I may not even imagine to further His purposes in the world.

THE ARTIST BELIEVES

"SCRIPTURE PRESERVES THE HEART'S CRIES IN LANGUAGE, IMAGES, AND MOVEMENTS SPACIOUS ENOUGH TO FIND OUR OWN EXPERIENCES." [3]

Before I am anything, against all odds, I am a believer. I believe in God; I believe Jesus is Truth, capital "T;" and the Spirit I talk about is the Holy one. Three in one, mystery and all. I believe that God speaks to us if we listen. As a photographer/theologian, I see and learn more about God through pictures.

Photographs are ways to share moments and expressions in life. Photography is a form of prayer, of hope. It teaches about the past, the now, and the future of God's great story and how we fit in. By its very nature, an image extends beyond the day. It preserves moments that no longer exist. It holds firm a memory of the way we used to be, and is a visual reminder that we are always transforming, changing, becoming.

Photography allows me to speak with intimate detail, clarity, authenticity, and emotion. This is how I approach life. My photographs are tributes to beauty in unusual places; sometimes they are discoveries that surprise. Perhaps that is because I have always placed value on things that others might consider valueless; or because I take delight in that which is often passed by without notice. Even as a child, I was the straggler, stooping down to notice the little things: a flower blooming from a concrete crack, a procession of ants carrying a stick, or blackberry branches sneaking under an old wooden fence.

Looking at the world, I find beauty that springs from contrast, or from the drama between light and dark, or old and new. Sometimes a simple intriguing texture captivates me. The poetry of the ordinary, the glow of simple, small elements, stirs me. My eye is drawn to the intimate details that make up the whole, or that point to hidden stories. I press the shutter when I experience this intimacy.

The moments I capture in faces are like short films on paper. In the pace of daily life, ordinary moments rush past us with rhythm, balance, and purity. These moments are rarely honored for their role in shaping us. In these faces, I see passion; I see triumph; I see greatness. The camera takes me to, and teaches me about, both the world I see and the world imagined. It allows me to share the intimate details on the journey of faith with all its twists and turns.

My journey with the lens--and, in fact, the daily living of life--is about discovering and rediscovering meanings. My expression sometimes brings revelations that lead to insight, to a memory, or toward understanding. When I take photographs, I better understand the world around me. And as my camera expresses the subject, I also reveal myself. Not only what I do, but who I am. Who I am becoming. I once heard a photographer say that the camera points in both directions. The pictures you see on the following pages reflect me as much as the subjects.

We all live our lives as editors, and even theologians. Every day we selectively view, hear, and experience, and this discretion forms the core of our beliefs and ideologies. We are shaped, or carved by them, just as the wind sculpts stone though you'd never imagine it possible.

Sometimes we choose our path in life. Sometimes it chooses us. Photography is both a part of my calling and takes me to, and teaches me about, the world I see and the world imagined. My prayer is that the world you see in this collection reveals something new about how God works and speaks, and about the untiring presence of the Spirit.

Never Alone   Joshua 1:5

PHOTOGRAPHY AS PARABLE

Truly, all my photographs are parables, anecdotes. They all have two stories--the one they tell in the viewer's mind, and the one I experienced while taking the shot. *The Salute* (page 23) has a power that explodes out of the frame. Both the shot and the story behind it are captivating. In fact, you might say that picture took me. After years of dreaming about traveling to Russia, I finally arrived in Moscow in May, 1996. Standing beneath St. Basil's Cathedral in Red Square the first possible moment I could, I glowed with the elation of experiencing Moscow's heartbeat. As it happened, hundreds of soldiers were milling around the square. I had not taken many shots of people up until then, and at first I was too nervous and intimidated to take pictures of people so closely. I walked hurriedly past them and all their prolific, though unintelligible (to me) comments.

As I circled the cathedral and Lenin's tomb, the desire to go back and take their photos grew stronger in me. It grabbed a hold of and overwhelmed me. Timidly, quickly, and with fear and trembling, I walked back behind dozens of trucks and quickly snapped eight pictures just as the soldiers were leaving. They are some of the best images I have taken. They capture the wildly diverse emotions of the soldiers as well as my own shyness and intrigue. Those soldiers will likely never know that they shared my initial, unforgettable, long-awaited and utterly delicious connection with Red Square and the domes of St. Basil, and that they were part of faith-filled steps to move beyond my comfort zone.

Pure Joy (page 11) also has a life of its own. When I first began working with Ernesto Mayans in his Santa Fe gallery, I had only printed roughly 150 of nearly 6,000 images. Our task was to weed through all the images and decide which ones to include in this first collection. After some correspondence regarding the project, the image I call *Pure Joy* came to me one night in a dream, and I awoke with it fresh in my mind's eye—even though I had not yet ever printed the image. It was one of thousands of sleeping images yet to wake up from my contact sheets. I love the unadulterated elation in that child. He is being chased by an adult who was catching and tickling the kid. Once caught, the child repeatedly and tirelessly, though out of breath, said, "Again," through infectious peals of giggles. The moment captured in that frame makes my soul smile.

"WHEN PHOTOGRAPHY IS GOOD, IT'S PRETTY INTERESTING, AND WHEN IT IS VERY GOOD, IT IS IRRATIONAL AND EVEN MAGICAL...IT HAS NOTHING TO DO WITH THE PHOTOGRAPHER'S CONSCIOUS WILL OR DESIRE. WHEN THE PHOTOGRAPH HAPPENS, IT COMES EASILY, AS A GIFT THAT SHOULD NOT BE QUESTIONED OR ANALYZED." PAUL STRAND [4]

The Plates

Pure Joy   1 Peter 1:8

Louisville, Kentucky, 1996

10

Peace   Philippians 4:7

Kathrin, Seligenstadt, Germany, 1996

Stiff-Necked   Exodus 32:9

Seligenstadt, Germany, 1996

The Olive Grove

Van Gogh's Olive Grove, San Remy, France, 1993

Junkyard Crucifix   1 Corinthians 1:18

Junkyard, Denver, Colorado, 1992

They Gathered 'Round   Mark 7:1

Friendly road side cows, Great Yarmouth, England, 1993

Sarah's Reaction   Genesis 18:12

Isabel, Seligenstadt, Germany, 1996

THEOLOGIAN AND PHOTOGRAPHER IN DIALOGUE

I am both theologian and photographer. Throughout my life, both sides have been in dialogue with each other. Sometimes, the photographer speaks about and seeks to understand theology; and sometimes the theologian uses pictures to see and know God more clearly and intimately, or to exegete [5] a text visually. In either case, it is like perceiving with a new dimension. Similar to reading a different version of the Bible and seeing something new, these pictures sometimes provide a new vision into Scripture.

Thinking about pictures and seeing in this fashion is a way to combine both my passion for God and for black and white photography. Where sometimes words limit or polarize us, imagery can help express the complex ideas, mysteries and beliefs inherent in theology, and they can draw us into the mystery.

Wonder and Awe   Exodus 15:11

"THE SUBCONSCIOUS PUSHING THROUGH THE CONSCIOUS,
TRYING TO LIVE IN THE LIGHT, IS LIKE THE SEED PUSHING UP THROUGH THE EARTH."
ALFRED STIEGLITZ [6]

PHOTOGRAPHY AS METAPHOR FOR SPIRITUAL LIFE

This verse says that the Lord shines his face on us. It is as if His countenance is being exposed onto us, just like the light shined onto a negative in the darkroom imprints the image onto photo paper and leaves a lasting impression. Have you ever wondered what are the "exposures" that are imprinting on your life? What brief flashes expose us to the image of God in our lives? What imprint is the Lord shining onto us? What about media's imprint on us?

In the ancient near East, the idea of holiness for the Hebrews contained the concept of having God's stamp on you, like a branded steer. This is similar to images that shine on us and imprint on our soul; and similar to what happens in the darkroom.

When you print photos in the darkroom, you have to start with darkness. In fact, it is absolutely necessary. I think the same is true spiritually. When we are in the darkest times, we have a hard time admitting that it is necessary. But thinking back over my life and the growth spurts, each one has involved a darkness, a desert experience. Some have been caused by my own choosing, some caused by God, some caused by chance, and some caused by the forces of darkness themselves. Each one, however, interacted with the light of Christ in me, to create beautiful contrast. Likewise, the most effective images are those that have intricate interaction between darkness and light. I think God teaches us the same thing in His Word.

Black and white photography is a beautiful interplay between light and darkness. The power of the two interacting creates the beauty—both in the darkroom and on the print. Sometimes in life, we are emotionally, spiritually, or intellectually in the dark, but those times often later reveal something that no other method would have been able to do. Transformation in and through darkness is a powerful, sustaining kind. And again, it is clear that the darkness is absolutely necessary. Have you ever wondered in what ways God is using the darkness in our lives to create beauty?

The Bible also says that we are "made in the image of God." Think about this: if it were true, then we should be able to see God in ourselves, in each other, and in the pictures we make of people that capture different stages of life. "The true light that gives light to every one came into the world," it says in John 1:9. Has Jesus imprinted you? Can you see it in your own image? What we do sheds light on our relationship to God and that light will shine in and through us as we focus on Him and on living like He says.

I can also think of specific times when images have imprinted on me. Henri Nouwen talks about this in *The Return of the Prodigal Son*, a book in which he describes a spiritual connection he has with Rembrandt's painting of the prodigal son parable from Scripture. "Rembrandt's embrace remained imprinted on my soul." [7] He admits to staring spellbound at the painting for hours, letting the images and the complex stories beneath them teach, guide and change him. And he finally admits that he does not know whether the parable leads him to see new aspects of the painting, or whether the painting leads him to discover new aspects of the parable. [8]

PHOTOGRAPHY AS PRAYER

"PHOTOGRAPHY IS A CERTAIN KIND OF LOVING." ERNST HAAS 9

A photograph is like a prayer. A picture is a way to connect with the sacred--sometimes ordinarily so--things of life. A photo allows us to discover and establish values and honor important moments and insights. It does not let us pass through life unaware. Taking, printing and viewing a photograph helps me uncover layers of my spirit so that I can grow closer to God. The best of my images penetrate with an untiring quest for, or brush with, truth.

The way I take photographs is very much like praying. It is an interaction, part of a relationship, something that works on me, changes me, teaches me. Sometimes it is simply a way I can praise. There are times when I just stop and listen, and capture what I hear or see. It is an intimate moment, and my sense is that those images that are portraits of prayer are the most powerful ones for others too. Prayer reflects the light of God, and with pictures, we can celebrate hints that the kingdom of God is at hand. I share signs of small joy that reveal the truth about the world. Maybe this is just one way that we can experience God this side of heaven. The whole process, though, teaches us how to see in fresh ways, which is a priceless gift.

I like to explore images that are portraits of truth. One way I do this is by showcasing details. I love the intimate textures that come from being up close. I love watching live theatre from the front row where you can see drops of sweat trickle down an actor's neck, or spit fly from their mouth as they speak. I love seeing the delicate detail at the center of a flower. I love the minutia of nature, the character that comes from wrinkles, and the intimacy of "up close." The process of taking pictures is one way to explore the details of how the sacred and the ordinary relate, and in many cases, they are the same thing. It is worth repeatedly asking what makes one thing sacred over another, and to revisit the dimensions of that question and how those qualities may change over time.

And Then God Speaks   Job 38:1

WHY PHOTOGRAPHY?

I never consciously set out to take pictures. It feels as if they started taking me. It is true, however, that I have always been a collector—of stories, of images, of experiences. I save memories of all kinds. And photography naturally became an avenue to collect the things I was seeing and learning, and even how I was changing. The camera is a great collector of ideas, stories, feelings, and sensed experiences.

Imagery can certainly have both positive and negative connotations, hugely powerful in either case. As with words, we carry a huge responsibility when we share thoughts with images. I believe that a picture can change your life. Pictures can challenge the sometimes banality, heaviness, or silliness of the world before it closes in on us. A picture can invite, and then inspire the viewer to see with fresh insight. It can require not only participation but also self-reflection. Think about the imagery of the crucifixion, or the stations of the cross in many Catholic churches. Michelangelo's Sistine Chapel. Those images are created and arranged to tell stories that change our life and our response to Christ.

Another thing that draws me to photography is that images often break down barriers where words may build them up. Especially when talking about theology and mystery, sometimes, when you get close to an idea it slips out of your hands like a greased pig at the county fair. When I first began to preach, I realized that sometimes an image can bring out a deeper meaning of a word or a concept. I also learned that sometimes when people may be closed to talking about God or faith, often times they will open up and share stories when they see a picture that touches them. Sometimes the baggage that comes with words in our common conversations about religion turns people off. When we speak about the inner world, the spirit, the light within, the kingdom of God—images can help us speak about these things. It is difficult to navigate the labels and automatic judgments that come with these words for some people. But being sensitive to the pain and limits of words gave me a chance to share my own stories of faith through pictures.

When you also realize that 70 percent of the world's population is not literate,[10] using pictures to communicate the Gospel takes on a whole new dimension. And let's not forget that Jesus did not write much. He taught using word pictures.

Iconography in the early development of the church in the 8th century became a way to include imagery and symbols as part of the visual language of earlier ages. Icons play less of a role in our visual vocabulary in the church today, but I stand on this tradition. Photography allows me to experiment with this visual vocabulary, as if I were using a different translation or version of the Bible to tease out intriguing nuances, or letting the light shine through the darkness as was the original intention of the early iconographers. We can learn much from the early artists in the church.

Yours is the Glory   1 Chronicles 29:11

The Salute

Red Square, Moscow, 1996

Search and Know Me   Psalm 139:23

Festival, Seligenstadt, Germany, 1993

To Remember   Joshua 4:7

Three Rocks, Silver Lake, California, 1996

Light and Dark   2 Samuel 22:29

Barn Door, Marin, California, 1993

Selah

Door Detail, Heidelberg, Germany, 1994

Childlike Faith   Matthew 18:3

Sarah, Louisville, Kentucky, 2001

My Presence is With You   Exodus 33:14

Bicycle and Castle, Burghausen, Germany, 1993

Rahab   Hebrews 11:31

Chinatown Doll, San Francisco, California, 1995

You Know My Thoughts   Psalm 139:2

George, Louisville, Kentucky 1996

Hallowed Be Thy Name

Bourbon Street, New Orleans, Louisiana, 1996

Everywhere I Go, I See You   Psalm 139:8

Annecy, France, 1993

Delight   Proverbs 23:24

Three Bikes, Amsterdam, Holland, 1995

All This is From God   2 Corinthians 5:18

Tulips, English Garden, London, 1996

Not My Will   Psalm 40:8

Man With Ladder, St. Petersburg, Russia, 1996

Fishers of Men   Mark 1:17

Hand Fishing, Capitola, California, 1995

The Overcomers I   Revelation 3:12

Outside the Hermitage, St. Petersburg, Russia, 1996

Integrity   Psalm 25:21

In the Middle of Wyoming, 1993

Once Cherished   Luke 16:15

Junk Chair, Junkyard, Denver, Colorado, 1992

What Lies Ahead   Philippians 3:13

Van Gogh's Sunflower field, outside Arles, France, 1993

Prayers of the Saints   Revelation 8:4

Van Gogh's Sunflower field, outside Arles, France, 1993

Still Waters   Psalm 23:2

Frozen Creek, Jackson Hole, Wyoming, 1993

Hope   Romans 5:4

Frozen Bushes, Jackson Hole, Wyoming, 1993

Some Things Are Hidden   Job 28:11

Underground Cryptoportique, Rheims, France, 1993

Do You Believe This?   John 11:26

Old Jewish Cemetery, Prague, Czech Republic, 1993

Russian Crosses   John 11:25

California Coast, Mendocino County, California, 1996

Turning Away   Deuteronomy 11:16

Frozen Branches, Jackson Hole, Wyoming, 1993

THE BLACK AND WHITENESS OF THE WORLD

THE DARKNESS IS ABSOLUTELY NECESSARY.

I never consciously considered shooting in color. Perhaps the black and whiteness, or rightness and wrongness, of the way I used to see the world affected my choice. When I was younger, I saw the world in black and white. I knew clearly. I saw distinctly. I loved the stark, crispness, exactness, and boldness of life. Perhaps that was my desire for certainty in a world full of change. Perhaps part of me still longs for that clarity, found in pictures, but blurred in the complexity of life.

Now I see infinite shades of grey—I see paradox, and I honor it. I appreciate layers, fuzzy boundaries, and images blending. Mysteries and doubts are now more comfortable. I think unanswered questions and complex messages are gorgeous, and I like they way they work in me like one of those fizzy tablets that bubble and dissolve in water.

The way I see the world has also changed throughout my life stages. It seems as though my life is punctuated with many identities. I have been blessed to have worked for twenty years in communications and leadership development in the high tech industry. I am a lifelong student of the Bible. I am a minister. I am a wife and new parent. I have passionately studied Theology and Social Ethics through a seminary master's program. I have co-written two business books. I play goofy games with my son. I photograph, teach, write, garden, paint. While these areas might seem to conflict, my life is actually a world of merged disciplines that support each other. My expressions are not only integrated; they inform and challenge each other. I worship when I take pictures; I speak not only with my mouth, but also with pen, computer, camera, and paintbrush. I minister through business, and as a wife and mother. In all I do, I consciously seek to tear down the compartments between our personal, work, and spiritual lives.

God speaks through me with all these tools. The message is the same though the medium may be quite different. The same quality found in my images is found also in my work life and ministry, my art, my theology journey, my relationships, and the ideas that lead me to what's next. Yet, I think that if I could explain exactly in words what I have taken in photographs, I would not have needed to take the picture.

When God is Silent   Job 13:3

I BELONG TO A FAMILY OF STORYTELLERS

As people of faith, God has provided us a grand and ongoing story in which to insert ourselves. In fact, God, the master storyteller, began the story by reaching down and speaking order into watery chaos. He enters history in the person of Jesus, and continues the story in our lives by sending us his Spirit. In his image, we are born natural storytellers.

My natural family is also rich with great storytellers. I loved my great Aunt, Tince we used to call her, who entertained us for hours with stories of my mother's family back to the 1800s. The hidden or forgotten details of our history were loaded with drama, innuendo, and crescendo. Tince never had far to go for a ready audience, especially during her last years in the retirement home.

My mother also enjoys center stage and remembers the most striking details that give punch to a story. One of the more brilliant women I know, she can synthesize many nuances in a situation. The strength of her faith not only inspires, but also astounds me. We share (as do my brothers and sisters) a deep faith and dependence upon God. Anything she touches is better for her having touched it.

And my father can spin a tale that will have the entire room gut laughing. He is simultaneously one of the funniest people and one of the deepest, heaviest thinkers I know. We are a family of superlatives. We do things "bigly," fully, intensely. He set this tone in our family. I am blessed to have inherited traces of faith, humor, depth, passion, and artistry from my parents.

Little did I know that my first camera would contribute to the storytelling legacy in my family. When I was eight, I dissected a generic pocket camera for the second grade science fair. I cut the device apart and mounted it just like a formaldehyde-soaked frog. I mounted the camera's back side firmly to the board and crudely connected a piece of yarn to each of its parts with a hand-written label

Undignified   2 Samuel 6:22

bearing its name. "Shutter." "Lens." "View finder." Though I would not really begin my photographic discourse until 15 years later, it seems that the tedious and intimate hours I spent with those specimen parts were to foreshadow the many hours I have spent and continue to spend with them to this day.

The camera has resurrected itself many times in my life. Trying to dissect it and understand how it works was as futile then as it is now. Even though I know technically what happens when the shutter opens, I often feel that spiritually the camera has more control over me than I do of it. One theme I see in my life is that though I may turn away or take a break from photography, or get too busy to devote the time I would like to it, photography continues to knock relentlessly on my door. It is as if the craft inevitably tracks me down and insists on using me as its instrument. I believe it is part of God's calling on my life, and perhaps my way to participate in and continue to share His stories.

LEARNING BY PHOTOGRAPHING

There certainly have been spiritless, dark, empty times in my life. Sometimes the loneliness in the desert parched more than my soul. The camera taught me at several times to see freshly--not only myself, but also stories and truth through the lens. At first, I experimented with the camera, and with seeing sides of me that had been hidden through young adulthood. Whether the camera was in front of my eye or not, I was learning to see differently. The Spirit was growing in me "like a seed pushing up through the earth," to borrow one of Steiglitz's metaphors. The camera has taught me to see differently.

I always wanted to be a writer. I'll never forget the interview for my first reporting job. Ten minutes into it, the editor gave me a writing assignment--I had four hours to interview a busy real estate executive, and then submit a story. Walking out the door I hear, "You know how to use a camera too, don't you?" as an intimidatingly complicated 35mm Canon was thrust into my hands. At that time, my only other experience with a camera was my second grade science fair dissection. I was required to submit pictures to accompany the story. Before I knew it, I was in an executive vice president's office taking notes and snapping pictures. When I arrived back at the magazine, to my horror I realized that while I thought I had taken a full roll of film, there was actually no film in the camera. Much of my technical photographic learning came in lessons like this. I was never formally trained, but admit that I learned the critical lessons in dramatic ways. Amazingly, I got that job, and for two years, the writer in me kept the photojournalist impostor side of me company.

A few years later, I learned to photograph artistically, and I began to watch my intuition and perspective come alive with the camera. It was as if I could see scenes and images on fire through the lens. Once again, I was seeing in new ways, watching the spirit unfold yet another layer. In 1992, I bought my first camera, a 35mm Nikon 5005. I shot my first personal artistic rolls of film in St. Thomas on a splurge vacation alone in the honeymoon capital of the world. One of the images in this collection is from that trip.

Travel has been a source of great growth and photographic material. In 1993, when I was 30, I quit my job, sold my car, and backpacked alone through Europe. During this time, pictures became an integral part of the way I communicated, thought, and experienced. In six months and 15 countries, I snapped over 4,000 images, behind which lie countless stories and events. Once again, it was as if the experiences took over, climbed inside and spoke to me, and told me what to photograph.

MY VIEW OF THE WORLD

God has given each of us a unique view of His world. I take pictures of both ordinary and extraordinary subjects. Some moments are quiet, common, everyday images. Some are once-in-a-lifetime gifts. I like high contrast, detailed texture, appropriate complexity, images pulsing with passion, and sublime expressions.

My quintessential style or photographic signature is "in-your-face" details. Superlatives. Tightly cropped faces, whether those belonging to buildings or people. An image that makes you ask questions, or finds a grin stealing across your face. An image that makes you say a great big "yes!" to it all. I never stage a photograph and always use natural light. Like unexposed film, I rarely have a preconceived notion of what the photo should be, though I admit that you won't find many sweeping panoramics on my contact sheets.

Photographs reveal my intensity. Like a young colt, or a pure beam of light, I know one speed and one intensity. My photographs reveal a tenacious spirit, an unquenchable thirst to learn and know truth and to live authentically. They reveal universality, and my hope to transcend with a language that does not box us in. They reveal a rich faithfulness, and an intuitiveness from details and nuances that tell a greater story. In sharing what most moves me, I reveal myself. But I never forget that I am part of a much larger drama.

I know that intensity can frighten people. I have learned to turn the volume down or perhaps soften a delivery, but harnessing my passion or energy is unnatural and often feels unethical. I struggle with this. Perhaps that will be the subject of another collection.

There are two sides of me. One side is drawn to photos of simple, striking, poetic grace. I love Paul Strand's pear and dishes. And Andre Kertesz' eyeglasses. And then there is the side of me that loves reflections of complexity, the simultaneous capture of contrasting emotions, or ironic depth. The desperate hopefulness of Walker Evans' subway snapshots, or of Dorothea Lange's social documentation. A great picture also tickles the other senses. Ernst Haas says, "Photography at its purest is a language of the senses." [11]

Terrifying times are those when my spirit is withered, assaulted, or just feels dead. When my spirit feels faded, it is all I can do to surrender my visions to God. I try to remember that faithfulness is called for precisely when hope is out of reach, unrealized, and perhaps even unrealizable. If I am being faithful only when goals are comfortably within reach, then perhaps I am living too small in my spiritual life. I am called to be hopeful, and faith-filled in sometimes hopeless situations. It is a non-negotiable part of the faith life. One of the most excruciating exercises I've learned is to surrender and to draw near to God even when it feels lonely. But what I've seen is that the feelings of drought and echoes of loneliness eventually pass. And there are times as I look back that the Spirit has often not faded, but rather my perception or my wholehearted engagement of it has.

MENTORS

No one single mentor or person has shaped and guided my life; rather I consider that I have a composite mentor, shaped over time, fashioned from both those living and those who have gone before me. As well, since my life is an integration of many disciplines, my mentors come from many places. I love the vision of the communion of saints, a gathering of diverse people who all offer visions and wisdom through the ages. I love learning from different types of people through the years. As a theologian exegeting with photos, I have some mentors from which I learn.

Auguste Rodin teaches about movement and space and capturing poignant, detailed expressions. Shakespeare and Chaucer magnify elements of human nature that we are often afraid to mention. Michelangelo knew how to capture gestures and nuances of God's grace like no other—in both paint and marble.

Spiritually, my calling is to live with Christ as my personal teacher. This alone is a life-long journey. Some of my co-disciples are Dietrich Bonhoeffer, Henri Nouwen, Abraham Heschel, Dallas Willard, Fredrich Buechner, Amadeus Mozart, Annie Dillard, Kathleen Norris, Anne Lammott, and many others too numerous to name. I learn from them. And Dr. Suess and my nine month old son help keep things in perspective. Not having a television allows room for interactions with these types of friends and their words, music, and art.

Photographically, I had taken pictures for years before I ever studied or learned from the masters. After taking nearly 6,000 images it was quite a shock to find out that I had shot images that some of the photography giants had taken in the 1940s—and I had never before seen their work! Edward Weston and Paul Strand both shot close ups of trees and rocks as subject matter, each on different coasts at the same time. My images from each coast follow suit. When I first saw Tina Modotti's Cala Lilies, I thought it was one of my images. Could this be one expression of the communion of saints?

Ernesto Mayans, a friend who owns an art gallery in Santa Fe, first taught me to believe in the force of the spirit in my images. I have learned and owe a great deal to him. In the life mentor category, I have learned from so many. My parents, many teachers and professors over the years. Fellow students. My husband Kevin and our little son, Joshua. One of my tennis coaches. A Catholic Priest, several pastors. My covenant friends Beth, Libby, Jan and Drew. Brett and Lyn, our ministry partners and life friends. The equip business missions teams. We are all rough stones getting smoother as we rub up against each other.

Word of God Speak   Psalm 139:7

Spirit in the Wall, Prague, Czech Republic, 1993

Crooked House

Stratford-Upon-Avon, England, 1993

Shrinkwrapped Christianity I

Storage Room, Musee St.-Denis, Rheims, France, 1993

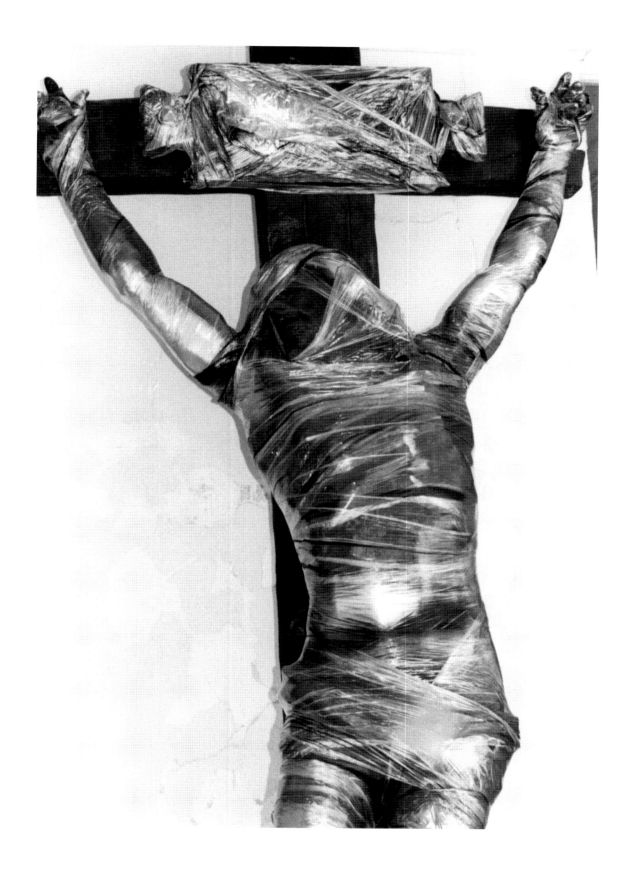

Peace Like a River   Isaiah 48:18

Santa Fe Walls, New Mexico, 1998

Jars of Clay I   2 Corinthians 4:7

Napa, California, 1996

Generations   Genesis 17:7

Pine Cones, Silver Lake, California, 1996

As We Forgive   Luke 11:4

Santa Fe Walls, New Mexico, 1998

David, The Goliath   1 Samuel 17:48

Michelangelo's David, Florence, Italy, 1993

Single Minded   Joshua 24:15

Agapanthus, Sausalito, California, 1996

Wisdom, Power and Love   Luke 1:17

St. Thomas, U.S. Virgin Islands, 1992

The Garment of Praise   Isaiah 61:3

Irina, Moscow Square, 1996

Too Amazing   Proverbs 30:19

Boy and Girl on Beach, Westport, Rhode Island, 1999

Fear No Evil   Matthew 10:26

Duomo Door Detail, Florence, Italy, 1993

I Have Redeemed You   Isaiah 44:22

Bench in Mist, Branson, Missouri, 1993

A Part of Me   John 14:20

Self Portrait in Reflective Object, KunstHaus Vien, Austria, 1993

Firm Footing   Psalm 40:2

Louisville, Kentucky, 1998

Prodigal Returns   Luke 15:20

Duck running on water, Silver Lake, California, 1996

The Last Shall Be First   Matthew 20:16

Russian Schoolchildren, Cathedral Square, Moscow, 1996

In You I Trust   Psalm 25:2

In the Middle of Wyoming, 1993

THE BEAUTY OF DARKNESS

"NO BLACK WITHOUT WHITE, WHITE WITHOUT BLACK. NO LIFE WITHOUT DEATH."
ALFRED STIEGLITZ [12]

We often see darkness as bad—something to stop. Often we think of evil or bad things as synonymous with darkness, and certainly there are many references in Scripture to support this. However, even Scripturally, darkness contains "beautiful" places. There is beauty in darkness that we often ignore, in life as well as in the Word. In fact, God is sometimes found there. In photography and in life, darkness is absolutely necessary. And often the interplay with the darkness is not only how we learn, but also what creates beauty. If we can accept it, we can see how utterly beautiful, peaceful, wonderful, and God-like the darkness can be.

Many Hebrew words indicate that darkness is evil, judgment or sin. But there are also words showing darkness as theophanies, or manifestations of God; secret hiding places for treasures; and dwelling places of God. In Isaiah, God says, "I will give you the treasures of darkness, riches stored in secret places, so that you may know that I am the Lord, the God of Israel, who summons you by name" (Isaiah 45:3). Here the darkness is like a jewel, a prize, a present, or something to be sought so that we may know God more personally.

God interacts with us in and through the darkness—both His and ours. "God sees the psalmist at all times, even in the dark, and he sees into the depths of his being, into his conscience--and that is no surprise since God was responsible for its creation." [13] This harkens back to the darkness in Genesis 1:2:

> "At the beginning of God's creating
> of the heavens and the earth,
> when the earth was wild and waste,
> darkness over the face of Ocean,
> rushing-spirit of God hovering
> over the face of waters-"
> (*The Schocken Bible, The Five Books of Moses*) [14]

Here God is found in the darkness, and it is a perfectly symmetrical order. The darkness is part of God and His order, it is where He is found, and from where He creates beauty. This vision of darkness completes the order of a world awaiting God's light—given in His image. Just like an image flashed on us or on film as in the darkroom.

In the next few verses in Genesis, we learn that God creates everything, even the darkness. "He called the light 'day,' and the darkness he called 'night'" (Genesis 1:5). Isaiah 45:7 reiterates this when God says, "I form the light and create darkness."

There is a dualism or contrast between light and darkness that is transcended and neutralized by Yahweh. [15]
Consider Psalm 139:

> "If I say, 'Surely the darkness will hide me
> and the light become night around me,
> even the darkness will not be dark to you;
> the night will shine like the day,
> for darkness is as light to you.'"

To God, all things are good. Even the darkness. For even in darkness, it is as light to the Lord. Even in darkness, his light shines, and dramatically so.

The Beauty of Darkness   Isaiah 45:3

"CHRISTIAN" ART

When Rainer Maria Rilke described one of Rodin's sculptures, he said, "This gesture makes a God necessary." [16] At its best, art enhances the relationship between people and God. It punctuates our faith and spiritual walk.

But this raises a question in my mind: "What is 'Christian art?'" Is that when everyone is decently dressed and represents Biblical figures? Free from blemishes? Absolutely not. Art that brings us closer to Christ, is a pathway to God, and teaches us about Jesus even without naming him is Christian art. Art that glorifies God, reflects his character, invites us into deeper relationship with him, and honors the paradoxes of our faith—that is Christian art.

Often in the church community we feel we have to stamp everything "Christian" and that that alone will make it edifying. We do ourselves and the Lord's work a disservice with this posture. And branding something religious does not make it automatically good. It is important to remember that only good art in the first place can be good sacred or religious art. Christian art, in fact, has no business being cheesy, tacky, sappy, or manipulative, though it sometimes seems that as believers we loosen our standards on the quality of our work or art. To really make an impact on the culture, we need to raise the standard and offer alternatives to the world's art that rival secular quality.

Good art that brings us into intimacy with Christ is a foretaste, like communion, of our partnership in eternity. In some ways, art contains the seed of the future. It points us, and prepares us—like the bread and wine—to a taste of the fullness of faith.

"In the very ability to make images there is a religious component. Powerful life can speak from a painting or statue, but in an image, it is as though the life were caught fast at a particular moment, as though motion were frozen." [17] Creativity is one of the ways we are made and share in the image of God. We owe a debt to the holiness of God to reflect his glory in our art expressions.

The relationship between art and theology offers one way that God is expressed to us. In this vein, imagery is a path to God and that which is sacred in our lives. Author Madeline L'Engle says, "It is not easy for me to be a Christian, to believe twenty-four hours a day all that I want to believe. I stray, and then my stories pull me back if I listen to them carefully. I have often been asked if my Christianity affects my stories, and surely it is the other way around; my stories affect my Christianity, restore me, shake me by the scruff of the neck, and pull this straying sinner into an awed faith." [18] I feel the same with the images in my portfolio. When I speak about them, it is not uncommon to have people, whether they know Christ or not, in tears as they bump into the truths of the Christian faith and how God works or how I've experienced him. Does Christianity affect art or does art affect Christianity? Or do they inform and sharpen each other?

BRANDING SOMETHING RELIGIOUS DOES NOT MAKE IT AUTOMATICALLY GOOD. ONLY GOOD ART IN THE FIRST PLACE CAN BE GOOD SACRED OR RELIGIOUS ART.

VISUAL EXEGESIS

"The Word is layered and cyclical and soul-filled in a way that validates our lives through the lens of the human drama." [19]

We worship an invisible God, and yet as followers of Christ, we spend our whole lives in relationship with Him, reaching for Him. Throughout the course of living a life sold out to Jesus, we seek whatever we can that will magnify or enrich our relationship with this God we can't see.

All of this, my history with the camera, my stories, my faith, my untiring quest for truth and more of God, have led me to a process I call "Visual Exegesis." [20] As both the theologian and the photographer side of me have been in dialogue over the past fifteen years or so, I have begun to experiment with Visual Exegesis, the process of using pictures to see and know God and to understand more about the paradoxes inherent in faith. Like using different translations, Visual Exegesis helps to see nuances in Scripture that we would not have otherwise seen. It helps us become more intimate with the questions, and to see fresh nuances and insights by visualizing messages or different layers in Scripture.

Exegesis is an extraction of meaning, an exploration of a Scriptural text based on methodologies and research to discover when, why, how, by whom, and for whom a piece of text was written. Its purpose is to learn the background elements of a text in order to interpret the text and draw out its meaning. Visual Exegesis, then, is a way to use photography to see another layer of what the text is saying. It is using a new vocabulary, or looking through another lens, literally, to see Scripture in pictures.

As I walk out my faith day by day, I weave in and out of themes. One theme in my current tapestry is that of mystery and paradox and ambiguity in a many-layered relationship with God. I am learning that I can't box God up, any more than I can systematize the Word He gives us. We can try and try, but in the end, the more we wrestle with the paradox part of our faith through spiritual disciplines, the more God smiles on us. In the midst of and facing great mysteries, I still choose to walk forward seeking Him. This is a major theme I am currently exploring through some classic spiritual disciplines. In conjunction with prayer, Scripture reading, conversations with other disciples, and journaling (my current disciplines), I have been experimenting with Visual Exegesis as a way to use imagery to help express these complex ideas, mysteries and beliefs where sometimes words limit or polarize us.

Exegesis is like digging for artifacts. You are in conversation with the Greek and Hebrew languages, literary resources, lexicons, form and structure, commentators, history, colleagues, and co-disciples about the relics in a passage of Scripture. Just like the scratches of Hebrew and Greek characters on parchment provide a tool to dig deeper, so too, does a photographic Visual Exegesis encourage us to use more senses to see new elements of Scripture. It is as if we are listening for, smelling, or touching the images in the text. Seeing Scripture in pictures, just like studying the ancient languages behind a text, shows things that we might otherwise miss. It can open up the text. Matthew Henry once said, "We cannot see the essence of God, but we see him in seeing by faith his attributes and perfections." [21] Perhaps this is similar to what David was thinking in Psalm 63 when he "beheld God's glory." Pictures can reflect God's character and his glory, and invite us deeper into His Word.

Visual Exegesis is powerful as an added exegetical tool, a way to hear what God is saying—and it is only possible after the rigorous work required to extract meaning from the text. Following time-honored exegetical methods, and after I have wrestled with a passage and written the sermon or message, then I pray for the Spirit to collaborate with me and choose the images that will tease out more meaning. I ask for illumination to choose images that reinforce or add new depth to a passage. Often it is as if the Spirit takes over and assembles the images and I get to watch.

THEOLOGY OF IMAGERY

Historically, I lean upon a rich lineage in which people have used imagery as way to see the sacred or to see God, and to connect with God's story. The heritage of religious iconography in Eastern and Russian Orthodox churches began in the early church a few hundred years after Christ. Over the centuries, icons played an important part in the liturgy of these churches because they were said to reflect the light of God.

In the 13th century, St. Bonaventure experimented with paintings and stained glass work as a spiritual discipline and a way to know God. He said, "All the arts and sciences are found to have points of contact in Scripture," [22] and he looked at the arts as parables or stories that reflected the heavenly process.

Michelangelo's Sistine Chapel, other great religious paintings and sculptures, iconography, and even Jesus' parables—these all represent imagery and symbols that were part of a visual language of earlier ages that are not as common in our current vocabulary. In exploring Visual Exegesis, I am experimenting with an old vocabulary in new ways. Visual Exegesis, therefore, and my leaning on black and white imagery, is in a sense, continuing the tradition of connecting into God's story visually—his story of choosing us, pursuing us, and holding fast to us century after century and through all time.

Where You Go, I Will Go   Ruth 1:16

CAUTION AGAINST "GOD MANUFACTURE"

There is a caution to this posture of creating art as a way to understand and commune with God. There is a caution against "God manufacture." [23] In other words, we owe a healthy distance and reverence to God in order to seek to understand Him. I can acknowledge, as Cynthia Ozick does, that "a transcendent God denies us a god of our own devising." [24] Definitely, in our limited humanness, we can not create a God in our graven images (or even in our own image) that comes close to the majesty, power and beauty that the real thing offers. Certainly I see this between the lines of God's whirlwind testimony in the book of Job.

Yet, I wonder: How can we use what we have been given by God to make sense of that same God when we can not see him? How can we make sense of God at all if we do not attempt to manufacture him in mechanisms, language and conversation that we understand and with the skills and talents we've been given? I concede that in our brokenness, we can not create or fully penetrate the way of God. But it is important to realize that we are able, even encouraged, to make sense of God with the capacities that he has given us. Is it "God manufacture" to create poetry, art, or writings that bring people (or only ourselves) closer to God? Quite the contrary, when we do, I believe God smiles on us.

As a photographer and a writer, I have said for years that my job is to get out of the way and let God speak through me. While I still believe that, I also wonder whether God has given me certain gifts so that I can experience God and his ways precisely because of what I have seen and what I have been given. Of course, I need to get my ego, self needs, and shadows out of the way so they don't poison the work, but as a communicator and artist, if my unique perception gets out of the way too much, I become yet another watered down Christian testimony that speaks to no one. I do not want to manufacture my own God by any means, but I do want to show my path, learning, and insight in approaching Him. I want to invite others to see what I see, wrestle with similar paradoxes, and to know God and me a little bit more through the process. My prayer is that the process of creation (manufacture?) brings me more intimate with God, and if God desires, others can also come closer. In my simple little way, this is approaching God's mystery with wonder, humility, and awe.

In *Phantom of the Opera*, there is a scene when Christine is under the Phantom's trance and sings delirious opera scales while looking into a larger-than-life mirror in her dressing room. At first, she sings to her reflection in the mirror, but as her scales escalate higher, her image in the mirror transforms into the Phantom. She then walks through the mirror into a new world. There is something mystical, and dare I say it, God-led, about surrendering my creative talents to God so that he can speak through them in a way that still reflects my personality and what he chooses to reveal through me. God made us in his image, and to create in his image, and to stay true to his Word and subordinate to Him through the process of creation.

"RELIGION AND ART STAND BESIDE EACH OTHER LIKE TWO FRIENDLY SOULS WHOSE INNER RELATIONSHIP, IF THEY SUSPECT IT, IS STILL UNKNOWN TO THEM." FRIEDRICH SCHLIERMACHER [25]

A PHOTOGRAPHIC CANON

I'm a collector of images and stories. I have been a black and white photographer for fifteen years, and a storyteller since I was a little girl. I believe God speaks to me through images and stories, and that he is also using stories and pictures to speak through me—to tell others about God.

I have a photographic canon of over 15,000 images captured from all over the world. Of these, I have printed roughly 400 prints in the darkroom, of which the 120 you see here are a subset. These pictures tell God's story through the lens of my life and images I have seen.

Photos have "taken" me all my life—I have said for years that I don't take pictures so much as they take me. In this way, the process is similar to prayer, preparing for a sermon, and surrendered communication in the spirit. Images are portraits of prayers, and as such, they reflect the light and contrast of God in life. My hope is to allow God to use the images, my life, joy, and creativity in ways I may not even imagine to further His purposes and for His glory in the world.

The Grass Shall Be Reeds and Rushes   Isaiah 35:7

You Are With Me   Psalm 23:4

Cemetery Pere Lachaise, Paris, France, 1993

Where Are You?   Genesis 3:9

Japanese Tea Garden, San Francisco, 1993

Down To The Grave   1 Samuel 2:6

Broken Tombstone, Cemetery Pere Lachaise, Paris, France, 1993

A New Song   Psalm 96:1

Tires, Georgetown, Colorado, 1992

Cup Overflowing   Psalm 23:5

Napa, California, 1995

The Shadows We Cast

Self Portrait on Bicycle, Bavaria, Germany, 1993

Not Me   Exodus 3

George, Louisville, Kentucky, 1996

To the Pure, All Things Are Pure   Titus 1:15

Tennessee Valley, California, 1996

You're All I Want   Acts 17:25

Wheel, Lakewood, Colorado, 1992

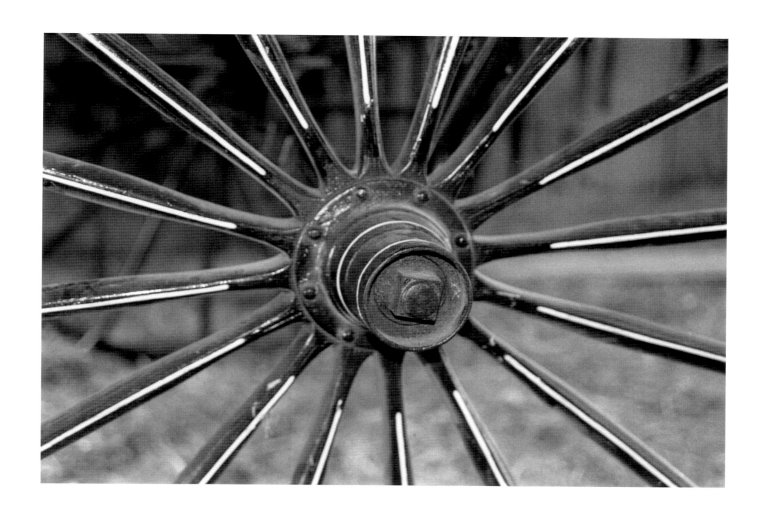

Cleanse Me   Psalm 51:2

California Coast near Capitola, 1995

Death's Loss   1 Corinthians 15:55

Curcifix With Broken Arm, Rheims, France, 1993

Faithful and True   Revelation 19:11

Carousel, Annecy, France, 1993

Eve   Genesis 3:6

Alleyway, Denver, Colorado, 1992

Genesis

German Schoolchildren, Seligenstadt, Germany, 1996

Crack in the Wall   Job 28:12

Alleyway, Denver, Colorado, 1992

Promised Land

Somewhere in Wyoming, Hale bays and tree, 1993

Castle Made of Sand   Matthew 7:26

Amsterdam Store Window, Holland, 1993

You Thought of Me   Romans 5:8

Crucifixion Silhouette, Cemetery, Vienna, Austria, 1993

Lead Me   Psalm 139:24

Trucks in the Middle of Wyoming, 1993

I Will Never Leave You   Deuteronomy 31:6

Two Boats, Camden, Maine, 1999

No High Heels

Amsterdam Wall, Holland, 1995

Hallelujah

Cathedral, near Moscow, 1996

Exodus

Moscow, 1996

Your Ways are Higher   Isaiah 55:9

Russian Domes, near Moscow, 1996

I Have Seen You in the Sanctuary   Pslam 63:2

California Coast near Half Moon Bay, 1994

The Eyes of All Israel 1 Kings 1:20

Ponte Vecchio Crowd, Florence, Italy, 1993

The Forgotten Ones   Psalm 9:18

Practice Statues Outside Michelangelo's David, Florence, Italy, 1993

Keeping Watch   Psalm 121:7

Cemetery Pere Lachaise, Paris, France, 1993

Whisper   1 Kings 19:12

Moscow Schoolchildren, Cathedral Square, Moscow, 1996

I Am With You   Isaiah 41:10

St. Petersburg Woman, 1996

The Lord is My Strength   Psalm 118:14

Russian Girl with Lion Statue, near St. Petersburg, 1996

Different Thoughts   Isaiah 55:8

Near Van Gogh's Sunflower Fields, Remy, France, 1993

Holy

Sheep on Path, Occidental, California, 1995

The Lord Reigns   Psalm 96:10

Moss on Redwoods, Marin, California, 1995

Shape Me   Job 10:8

Fortress, Les Baux, France, 1993

Obedience   Leviticus 26:1

Inside the Ring of Stones, Stonehenge, England, 1996

The Last Hour   Mark 14:37

Florence Gelato Shop, Italy, 1993

Refine Me   Malachi 3:3

Women Relief, near Seligenstadt, Germany, 2000

Above All Wisdom   Ephesians 1:9

Chess Players, Norwich, England, 1993

Different Gifts, Same Spirit   1 Corinthians 12:4

Budapest, Hungary, 1993

Joyful Saints I   Psalm 68:3

Redwoods, Muir Woods, California, 1993

Worship   Psalm 63:4

Louisville, Kentucky, 1998

Deuteronomy

New Orleans Window, Louisiana, 1996

Innocence   Matthew 18:5

Joshua, Two Weeks Old, 2004

My Master, My Lord   Matthew 15:27

Buckets, Farm Near Denver, Colorado, 1992

Touch of Hope   Romans 8:24

Ponte Vecchio Shutters, Florence, Italy, 1993

Almighty

Near Capitola, California, 1995

Work of Your Fingers   Psalm 8:3

Rodeo Beach, Marin, California, 1996

Here Am I   Genesis 22:1

Peacock, Vienna, Austria, 1993

Where Can I Go?   Psalm 139:7

Erik and George, Louisville, Kentucky, 1998

Good News From a Distant Land   Proverbs 25:25

Russian Soldier, Cathedral Square, Moscow, 1996

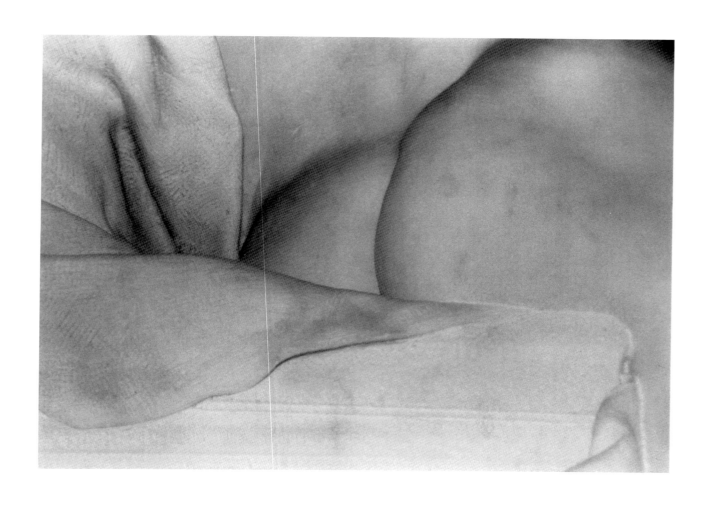

Adam   Genesis 2:7

Gold Room Statue, Musee D'Orsay, Paris, France, 1993

Far Side of the Sea   Psalm 139:9

Big Sur, California, 1995

Mourning　　　Psalm 38:6

Cemetery Pere Lachaise, Paris, France, 1993

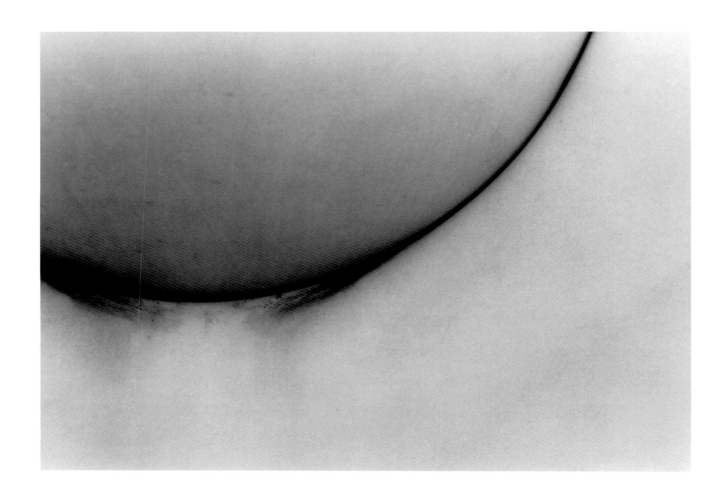

Tomb

White Marble Tombstone, Salzburg, Austria, 1993

Immeasurably More   Ephesians 3:20

Ladder and Thatch Roof, Swellendam, South Africa, 2003

Upside Down   Isaiah 29:16

Virginia Beach, Virginia, 1994

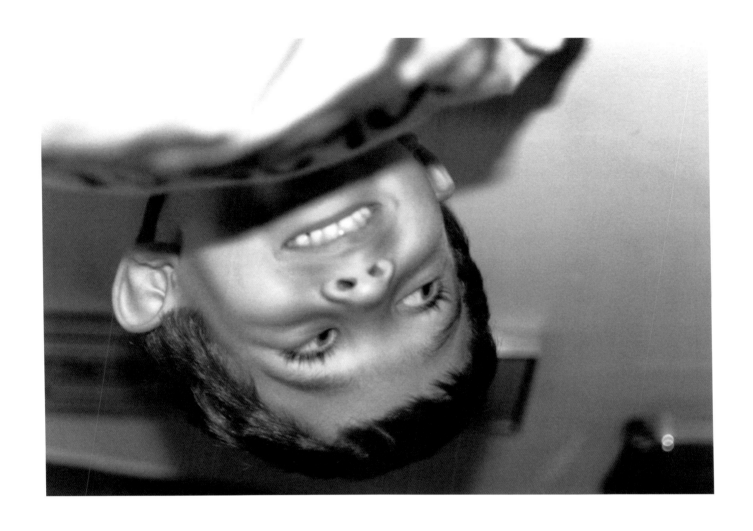

ACKNOWLEDGMENTS

A Joyful Sound

We are who we are because of who surrounds us. I am surrounded by a great cloud of partners and friends who helped bring this book out of its hidden state onto these pages. I am grateful to so many who have contributed to this project in all kinds of ways. There have been many who encouraged me to complete this book and who have been a strong support when I lost steam. They enhance the force of the spirit in my life.

My parents, brothers, sister, and their spouses have always believed in me. My friends and encouragers are also part of this collection and I am grateful to: Brett and Lyn Johnson, Mike Putlock, Bob and Cindi Norsworthy, Jonathan and Jennifer Campbell, Kim and Virendra Vase, Sharon Sterling, Beth Fraker, Curt Longacre, Drew Banks, Gail Doering, Libby Vincent, Dwight Morita, Jan Tyler Bock, Ernesto Mayans, Dr. Samuel Lee, John Olsen, Pat Nolan, Rob Johnston, Dr. Richard Mouw, Anita Schiller, Graham and Diane Vermooten.

My husband, Kevin, is my partner in immeasurable ways. He inspires and supports me to be more than I am alone. I am blessed by him in my life and his presence is part of this collection. Our nine-month old (as I write this) son, Joshua, inspires me at every turn. His fingerprints are even in these pages.

Father, Son and Spirit, you are the reason I am. Above all, I thank you.

REFERENCES/END NOTES

1 Dietrich Bonhoeffer, *Letters and Papers from Prison*, Touchstone, New York, 1971, pgs 279-282. Pastor and theologian Bonhoeffer talks about a "religionless" Christianity where believing people focus less on the religion of Christianity and more on the foundational truths of it.
2 *Harry Callahan*, Little Brown and Company, Canada, 1996, p 35.
3 *The Psalms*, Riverhead Books, New York, 1997, p x.
4 *Paul Strand Sixty Years of Photography*, Aperture, New York, 1976, p 173.
5 Exegesis: an explanation or critical interpretation of a text. "Exegesis investigates and expresses the true sense of sacred Scripture." (From the *New Advent Encyclopedia*). I explain about the process of Visual Exegesis on page 82.
6 Dorothy Norman, *Alfred Stieglitz: An American Seer*, Aperture, New York, 1960, p 16.
7 Henri Nouwen, *The Return of the Prodigal Son*, Image Books, New York, 1994, p 5.
8 Ibid, p 54.
9 *Ernst Haas In Black and White*, Little Brown and Company, Canada, p 17.
10 Charles Kraft, *Communication Theory for Christian Witness*, Orbis Books, New York, 2000, p 120.
11 *Ernst Haas In Black and White*, Little Brown and Company, Canada, p 15.
12 Dorothy Norman, *Alfred Stieglitz: An American Seer*, Aperture, New York, 1960, p 229.
13 Leslie Allen, *Word Biblical Commentary, Psalms 101-150*, Word Books, Texas, 1983, p 261.
14 Dr. Everett Fox, *The Schocken Bible, The Five Books of Moses*, Random House, New York, 1983, p 9.
15 Leslie Allen, *Word Biblical Commentary, Psalms 101-150*, Word Books, Texas, 1983, p 251.
16 Rainer Maria Rilke, *Rodin*, Peregrine Smith, Inc, Utah, 1979, p 65.
17 Gerard van der Leeuw, *The Holy in Art–Sacred and Profane Beauty*, Holt, Rinehart and Winston, New York, 1963, p 155.
18 Madeleine L'Engle, *Walking on Water*, Northpoint Press, New York, 1980, p 106.
19 *The Psalms*, Riverhead Books, New York, 1997, p xiv.
20 Visual Exegesis is a phrase I coined in July, 1999 to describe the process of using imagery to learn more about or to extract more meaning from a passage of Scripture.
21 Gerard van der Leeuw, *The Holy in Art–Sacred and Profane Beauty*, Holt, Rinehart and Winston, New York, 1963, p 193.
22 Ibid, p 83.
23 Cynthia Ozick, Preface to *The Book of Job*, Random House, New York, 1998, p xxiii.
24 Ibid.
25 Gerard van der Leeuw, *The Holy in Art–Sacred and Profane Beauty*, Holt, Rinehart and Winston, New York, 1963, p 189.

PHOTO SCRIPTURES

The following verses are from the New International Version of the Bible.

Page 2, *Teach Me* Psalm 25:4
Show me your ways, oh Lord, teach me your paths.

Page 7, *Never Alone* Joshua 1:5
No one will be able to stand up against you all the days of your life. As I was with Moses, so I will be with you; I will never leave you nor forsake you.

Page 11, *Pure Joy* I Peter 1:8
Though you have not seen him, you love him; and even though you do not see him now, you believe in him and are filled with an inexpressible and glorious joy.

Page 12, *Peace* Philippians 4:7
And the peace of God, which transcends all understanding, will guard your hearts and your minds in Christ Jesus.

Page 13, *Stiff-Necked* Exodus 32:9
"I have seen these people," the Lord said to Moses, "and they are a stiff-necked people."

Page 14, *The Olive Grove*

Page 15, *Junkyard Crucifix* I Corinthians 1:18
For the message of the cross is foolishness to those who are perishing, but to us who are being saved it is the power of God.

Page 16, *They Gathered 'Round* Mark 7:1-2
The Pharisees and some of the teachers of the law who had come from Jerusalem gathered around Jesus and saw some of his disciples eating food with hands that were "unclean," that is, unwashed.

Page 17, *Sarah's Reaction* Genesis 18:12
So Sarah laughed to herself as she thought, "After I am worn out and my master is old, will I now have this pleasure?"

Page 18, *Wonder and Awe* Exodus 15:11
"Who among the gods is like you, oh Lord. Who is like you—majestic in holiness, awesome in glory, working wonders?

Page 20, *And Then God Speaks* Job 38:1
Then the Lord answered Job out of the storm.

Page 21, *Yours is the Glory* I Chronicles 29:11
Yours, oh Lord, is the greatness and the power and the glory and the majesty and the splendor, for everything in heaven and earth is yours. Yours, oh Lord, is the kingdom; you are exalted as head over all.

Page 23, *The Salute*

Page 24, *Search and Know Me* Psalm 139:23
Search me, oh God, and know my heart; test me and know my anxious thoughts.

Page 25, *To Remember* Joshua 4:7
These stones are to be a memorial to the people of Israel forever.

Page 26, *Light and Dark* 2 Samuel 22:29
You are my lamp, oh Lord; the Lord turns my darkness into light.

Page 27, *Selah* Psalms

Page 28, *Childlike Faith* Matthew 18:3
And he said: "I tell you the truth, unless you change and become like little children, you will never enter the kingdom of heaven."

Page 29, *My Presence is With You* Exodus 33:14
The Lord replied, "My presence will go with you, and I will give you rest."

Page 31, *Rahab* Hebrews 11:31
By faith the prostitute Rahab, because she welcomed the spies, was not killed with those who were disobedient.

Page 32, *You Know My Thoughts* Psalm 139:2
You know when I sit and when I rise; you perceive my thoughts from afar.

Page 33, *Hallowed Be Thy Name*

Page 34, *Everywhere I Go, I See You* Psalm 139:8
If I go up to the heavens, you are there; if I make my bed in the depths, you are there.

Page 35, *Delight* Proverbs 23:24
The father of a righteous man has great joy; he who has a wise son delights in him.

Page 37, *All This Is From God* 2 Corinthians 5:17-18
Therefore, if anyone is in Christ, he is a new creation; the old has gone, the new has come! All this is from God, who reconciled us to himself through Christ and gave us the ministry of reconciliation.

Page 39, *Not My Will* Psalm 40:8
I desire to do your will, oh my God; your law is within my heart.

Page 40, *Fishers of Men* Mark 1:17
"Come, follow me," Jesus said, "and I will make you fishers of men."

Page 41, *The Overcomers I* Revelation 3:12
Him who overcomes I will make a pillar in the temple of my God.

Page 110, *Hallelujah*

Page 111, *Exodus*

Page 112, *Your Ways Are Higher*   Isaiah 55:9
"As the heavens are higher than the earth, so are my ways higher than your ways, and my thoughts than your thoughts."

Page 113, *I Have Seen You in the Sanctuary*   Psalm 63:2
I have seen you in the sanctuary and beheld your power and your glory.

Page 114, *The Eyes of All Israel*   I Kings 1:20
My Lord the king, the eyes of all Israel are on you, to learn from you who will sit on the throne of my Lord the king after him.

Page 115, *The Forgotten Ones*   Psalm 9:18
But the needy will not always be forgotten, nor the hope of the afflicted ever perish.

Page 116, *Keeping Watch*   Psalm 121:7
The Lord will keep you from all harm—he will watch over your life.

Page 117, *Whisper*   I Kings 19:12
After the earthquake came a fire, but the Lord was not in the fire. And after the fire came a gentle whisper.

Page 118, *I Am With You*   Isaiah 41:10
So do not fear, for I am with you; do not be dismayed, for I am your God. I will strengthen you and help you; I will uphold you with my righteous right hand.

Page 119, *The Lord is My Strength*   Psalm 118:14
The Lord is my strength and my song; he has become my salvation.

Page 121, *Different Thoughts*   Isaiah 55:8
"For my thoughts are not your thoughts, neither are your ways my ways," declares the Lord.

Page 122, *Holy*

Page 123, *The Lord Reigns*   Psalm 96:10
Say among the nations, "The Lord reigns." The world is firmly established, it cannot be moved.

Page 124, *Shape Me*   Job 10:8
Your hands shaped me and made me.

Page 125, *Obedience*   Leviticus 26:1
"Do not make idols or set up an image or a sacred stone for yourselves, and do not place a carved stone in your land to bow down before it. I am the Lord your God."

Page 126, *The Last Hour*   Mark 14:37
Then he returned to his disciples and found them sleeping. "Simon," he said to Peter, "are you asleep? Could you not keep watch for one hour?"

Page 127, *Refine Me*   Malachi 3:3
He will sit as a refiner and purifier of silver; he will purify the Levites and refine them like gold and silver. Then the Lord will have men who will bring offerings in righteousness.

Page 129, *Above All Wisdom*   Ephesians 1:9
And he made known to us the mystery of his will according to his good pleasure, which he purposed in Christ.

Page 130, *Different Gifts, Same Spirit*   I Corinthians 12:4
There are different kinds of gifts, but the same Spirit.

Page 131, *Joyful Saints I*   Psalm 68:3
But may the righteous be glad and rejoice before God; may they be happy and joyful.

Page 132, *Worship*   Psalm 63:4
I will praise you as long as I live, and in your name I will lift up my hands.

Page 133, *Deuteronomy*

Page 134, *Innocence*   Matthew 18:5
And whoever welcomes a little child like this in my name welcomes me.

Page 135, *My Master, My Lord*   Matthew 15:27
"Yes, Lord," she said, "but even the dogs eat the crumbs that fall from their masters' table."

Page 136, *Touch of Hope*   Romans 8:24
For in this hope we were saved. But hope that is seen is no hope at all. Who hopes for what he already has?

Page 137, *Almighty*

Page 139, *Work of Your Fingers*   Psalm 8:3-4
When I consider your heavens, the work of your fingers, the moon and the stars, which you have set in place, what is man that you are mindful of him, the son of man that you care for him?

Page 139, *Here Am I*   Genesis 22:1
The Sacrifice of Isaac. Some time later God tested Abraham. He said to him, "Abraham!" "Here I am," he replied.

Page 141, *Where Can I Go?*   Psalm 139:7
Where can I flee from your presence?

Page 142, *Good News From a Distant Land*   Proverbs 25:25
Like cold water to a weary soul is good news from a distant land.

Page 143, *Adam*   Genesis 2:7
The Lord God formed the man from the dust of the ground and breathed into his nostrils the breath of life, and the man became a living being.

Page 144, *Far Side of the Sea*   Psalm 139:9-10
If I rise on the wings of the dawn, if I settle on the far side of the sea, even there your hand will guide me, your right hand will hold me fast.

Page 145, *Mourning*   Psalm 38:6
I am bowed down and brought very low; all day long I go about mourning.

Page 146, *Tomb*

Page 147, *Immeasurably More*   Ephesians 3:20
Now to him who is able to do immeasurably more than all we ask or imagine, according to his power that is at work within us, to him be the glory.

Page 149, *Upside Down*   Isaiah 29:16
You turn things upside down, as if the potter were thought to be like the clay! Shall what is formed say to him who formed it, "He did not make me"? Can the pot say of the potter, "He knows nothing?"

Page 150, *A Joyful Sound*